A Memoir of Heartbreak

By:

Victoria D'Ariano

<u>Dedications</u>:

Thank you to those who showed me love and
kindness through my darkest of days

About the Author

Victoria D'Ariano was born and raised in London, Ontario with her parents and two siblings Alex and Laura. After earning her Honors degree in Kinesiology from Western University, Victoria spent time using her love for the sport to embed herself in the fitness world, finding her path and her voice through her experiences and connections. Victoria uses her writing and open-form poetry to express the feelings and emotions experienced by many individuals throughout life, whether as a collective or individually, and hopes to open doors for those who feel vulnerable during these times

Contents

Crashing Down

I see a text.
My heart starts to race.
Suddenly I can't breathe.
I collapse.
It's all been a lie.
My gut wrenches, but deep down I think I knew.
I chose not to believe; how could it be true?
I always thought I'd be with you.
My world comes crashing down.
My heart aches, it shatters.
Blood drips,
From the knife sticking in my back.
How could you?
How could you do this to me?
I made promises.
You told lies.
A part of me dies.
I'll have to start over,
And I'll be strong.
I pick myself up,
I carry on.

I Vowed

I vowed to forever loving you,
You looked me in the eyes, and said I do.
Years, we built a life.
Now I know it was built on lies.
I'm not perfect, nor will I pretend to be.
I have my faults, I'm a human being.
But I tried, I really tried.
I gave you all of me,
You sucked me dry.
My world revolved around you, but yours didn't
care about mine.
You, you, you all the time.
You never told me how you felt.
How can I fix something I know nothing about?

Ashes

Flames.
All around.
All we built,
Burnt down to the ground.
Ashes are all that's left,
Smoke filling your lungs.
Coughing.
You can't breathe?
Now you know what it's like to be me.

13

You are talking.
But,
I don't hear a word.
I am 13 years old again.
In the Swiss Chalet bathroom.
Tears running down my cheeks.
Feeling the stall walls closing in on me.
Trying to catch my breath
As they squeeze me.
Just trying to breathe.
Gasping for air.
In that moment,
I am 13 years old again.

Sirens

I'm sobbing.
My heart starts racing.
I'm breathing so fast.
Look at me they say,
Just breathe.
I can't slow it down.
I see black.
Then I'm back.
Look at me they say,
Oh, I try.
Now I'm gone so far away.
Thick black from my mind to my body.
I try to move,
But I can't.
I'm paralyzed.
I tell myself to speak, even just a whisper.
Don't let them worry, just give them a word.
Oh, I try.
The ambulance takes me away,
I'm so exhausted, I'm losing the fight.
I hear my name.
I feel the pain.
They say look at me,
Oh, I try.

Sleep

Sleep.
You suddenly became my enemy.
I went to sleep with a baby inside,
And woke up to blood.
Goodbye.
Sleep.
I went to sleep a wife,
And woke up to lies.
Sleep.
I stayed awake for weeks.
Because anytime I'd close my eyes,
I'd forget.
Until I woke up,
And it would hit me like the first time.
Sleep.
You've become
My enemy.

<u>Slipping</u>

You took her hand,
Instead of holding mine.
I was your person,
You were mine.
My mind won't stop,
You and her,
Is all I see.
I wish I could rewind time.
You'd tell me how you felt,
We'd work through the hurt,
The pain.
I felt you slipping,
But I trusted you.
I had thoughts,
But I told myself it couldn't be true.
Now I know I was too stupid, and naive.
I want to be angry, but all I feel is sad.
The life we built, the love we had.

__Gone__

I needed you,
I felt alone,
So lonely.
You were nowhere to be found.
You were already gone.

<u>Naked</u>

Your skin on hers
Your lips on hers
You inside,
Her.
Not me.
Her.

Expressionless

Belittled, lied to, and betrayed.
Used my mental health to get your way,
Manipulation to convey.
It's not easy for me to walk away,
My mind spins with thoughts,
That won't stop.
I have to keep going,
I start to walk.
You stare as I go.
An expressionless face.
I'll never know your feelings,
Your thoughts.

A Loss

The loss of the baby,
I never had.
Get over it.
I'd hear.
So, I tried.
But it was real,
Real to me.
The pain I felt.
The grieving I had to do.
I had so much to be grateful for.
I knew that, but it didn't take the hurt away.
You made me feel bad,
For the feelings I had.
It was my body,
My pain.
Not yours to dismiss.
Not yours to bury.
You could have shown me love and kindness,
You could have listened to me.
Did I have to scream?
You didn't get it, but did you ever really try?
You never even asked me why.
Instead,
You carved the wedge,
That was placed between you and I.

A Mother

A mother,
All I wanted,
To be.
After the loss,
The desire grew deeper,
It consumed me.
I couldn't control the anger I had,
The animosity.
I wanted the big round belly,
The life inside.
I couldn't be around others,
As the pain was too dark.
I didn't like who it made me,
But I couldn't push it aside.
I thought a baby would save me,
Save me from my sad mind.
Make me happy again,
When each month,
It'd come.
And I'd cry.
I know it was too much for you.
As, it was too I.

A Date

Sometimes I feel stupid,
For the love I had.
You were my all,
My
Everything.
I didn't know how much it could hurt,
When the love stopped being returned.
My love was real, and deep.
I thought we had forever,
A love story that wouldn't end.
Kids
Grandchildren
And years of memories
To look back upon.
Wrinkles, grey hair, and getting old.
I can hear my vows,
Oh, they were honest and true.
It only feels like yesterday,
That I spoke them to you.
Somehow the love became undone.
I wish I could figure out why,
But it wouldn't change the outcome.
Our anniversary is now just a date,
One that we will both forget,
Someday.

Questions

I keep questioning my worth.
I keep questioning my love,
Was it not enough?
You had my whole heart,
But maybe it wasn't big enough.
So many questions,
And thoughts in my mind.
Rethinking everything,
What could I have changed?
What could I have done,
So, you didn't fall out of love?

Mirror On The Wall

Look in the mirror,
What do you see?
Honestly?
Yes honestly.
I see a failure.
All I see is failure.
It's written all over me.
Failed wife.
Failed mother.
Failed dreams.
Failure,
Failure,
Failure
Is
All
I
See.

<u>Honesty</u>

The words I write aren't supposed to be mean.
The words I write come from my heart,
Pure honesty.
The things I feel,
Pour out of me.
My thoughts,
My feelings.
My writing isn't perfect,
Just like me.
But I give them my heart and all of my honesty.

Seams

I don't think you understand how hard it is for me
to see,
You living your life like nothing happened,
While I'm falling apart at the seams.
How can I be so broken?
While you seem so, okay?
Is my love that much stronger?
Or did yours already fade away?
I'm here just trying to survive,
While you continue to thrive.
Was it all an act, so that I'd stay by your side?
Did you ever really love me?
Was any of it not a lie?
How can you be so calm?
While I'm dying inside.
While you continue to be,
So alive.

<u>Scars</u>

Being broken is a chance to restart,
You get to pick up the pieces,
And dust them off.
You get to put yourself back together,
Stronger than before.
You'll have scars,
Which ensures you don't forget.
Never letting yourself endure what you don't
deserve.
You'll learn from this,
As painful as it may be.
This will be an opportunity.

Rare Woman

I have a good heart,
That's always been true.
I'm rare,
And one day you'll see.
You'll always be searching for the rare woman you
gave away.
You'll crave the deepness of the love I gave.
You'll yearn for the loyalty,
And security.
You'll feel forever empty,
A part missing from where I used to be.
A rare woman,
I'll always be.

Love & Hate

I never understood how you could
Love and hate
Polar opposites,
Two conflicting emotions.
Two extremes.
Both so strong,
Both so raw.
I understand it now.
The love is still there,
But the hate keeps growing inside,
Deeper and stronger.
As days pass by.

Stupid Girl

I'm so angry,
Angry all the time.
I want to scream
I want to cry.
All the betrayal floods my mind.
My face turns red,
I start to sting,
Body tingling.
Heart racing.
Pretending to be my friend
Yet knowing the truth.
Choosing to keep the secrets,
The lies.
I was a big joke,
In your eyes.
I can see you all laughing.
Ha, ha, ha,
Stupid girl,
And,
You
Were
Right.

<u>Never Again</u>

Never again,
Will
You
Have
Me.
Never again,
Will
You
Break
Me.

Sacred & Special

All the places,
That were mine.
Sacred and special,
You had to,
Take away.

Funeral

I stand in black,
Mourning.
Mourning you.
You aren't dead,
But it's still a loss.
No more hugs,
Kisses,
And I love you.
This is the worst pain I've ever felt.
Never did I think,
I'd be mourning over you.
Never did I think I'd have to say goodbye,
While you were,
Still alive.

__Smile__

Smile,
Smile, beautiful girl.
You have so much light.
You are still shining,
You just can't see.
So much to give.
So much more to live.
You will be okay,
I promise you that.
Yes,
It's going to hurt.
For a long time,
It will be a fight.
You will wonder how to carry on.
But,
You will.
I promise you that.
Please,
Never stop smiling.
You have so much more,
Much more,
To live for.

Trash

You wanted it all,
Whatever price it took.
Including losing me,
And sadly,
You didn't think twice.
I was no longer your love,
Just a piece of trash,
You crumpled,
And
Threw
Away.

Anxiety

The knot in my stomach,
The lump in my throat.
The tightness of my chest.
I feel sick,
Nauseous.
I can't eat,
I can't sleep.
Breathing feels hard.
The shallow breaths.
The racing thoughts,
Please,
Please stop.
Anxiety,
I can't keep living with you.

Pieces

Each piece I gave,
I realized,
Was a piece I lost of me.
You climbed to the top,
Piece by piece.
While
I was,
Buried beneath.

Worthy

You don't deserve this I tell myself.
You are worthy, you are kind.
You will be loved again.
The pain will subside.
I miss you,
Whoever you are.
I promise myself to keep going,
One foot in front of the other.
My legs feel heavy,
I'm broken, but I won't stop.
Keep moving forward I continue to say.
I won't give up.
This won't be my outcome.

Your Dreams

When we first met,
You had a dream.
We lived our lives to make it come true.
We worked and worked,
Getting you closer and closer.
We started from the bottom,
And looked up to the top.
Big, eager eyes,
And hearts full of hope.
We climbed,
And climbed.
One step at a time.
We did it together,
Don't you remember?
We were a team,
Or so I thought.
You've now made it to the top,
Your dreams have come true.
But now that you're there,
All you see is the view.
You forget where we started,
Those who helped and supported you.
No one makes it to the top alone,
I think you forgot.
You didn't carry all the weight.
Years I devoted,
So, your dreams could come true.
Somehow, you've forgotten,
How much I helped you.
No use for me now.
I'm pushed away,

I'm back at the bottom,
Looking up at you.
You're standing tall.
While I feel so small.

House

It's just a house.
I keep telling myself.
I know it's true,
But I can't stop thinking.
About me, and you.
The years of hard work,
To get those keys.
It was the start of something beautiful,
Our future, our dreams.
I had a vision of what it would be.
So much to look forward to,
So much more for us to be.
The boys by their window,
Sunbathing.
It was our home.
Oh, the peace I felt.
Now as I pack it up,
I can't seem to believe it.
Only one year ago did we get the keys.
Only one year ago did our future seem so bright,
So promising.
Soon I'll leave.
And our home will become a house,
And that's all it will ever be.

Boxes

Our story,
Our future.
Packed away.
Left to collect dust.
And be forgotten.

I Hate This

I hate this.
I hate how you're no longer the one.
My person.
I feel I didn't get a choice in this,
Yet the damage is done.
I hate that when I grab my phone
I want to text you,
And ask about your day.
I hate that I can't stop thinking about you,
About us.
About what we would have become.
I hate that I still love you,
Even after what you've done.
I hate how we didn't get our forever,
And now I'm left, broken and alone.
I hate you for what you did.
To me,
To you,
To us.

Dear 2020

Dear 2020,
You are a year I'll never forget.
The start of you,
I was dealing with a loss.
That took a little bit of me.
That took a long time to heal,
Physically,
And mentally.
With emotions, I couldn't control.
Dear 2020,
Was it not enough?
You decided my heart had to break even more.
Another loss.
I didn't think I'd make it through.
The times I couldn't breathe,
Passing out due to the hyperventilating.
But you tested me and tested me,
Because you knew my strength.
You weren't going to give up on me.
Like I wasn't going to give up on myself.
In so much hurt,
I felt strength.
In so much darkness,
I felt the light.
Each time you tore me down,
I continued to get up.
Each time you broke me,
I put myself back together.
2020, I now know why
You did what you did.
You were making me into a warrior.

And 2020,
You did.

The Knife

The pain you put me through
Is too extreme to write.
I can't quite articulate the way you took the knife
and sliced.
But I will try,
So here it goes.
You took my kindness and strangled its throat.
You took my loyalty and stabbed it deep.
You took my love and buried it beneath.
You took my light and burnt it out.
You took my heart and threw it so hard,
It shattered,
Into so many pieces.
Now scattered,
All around.

A Vague Dream

It takes a moment,
For the life you know to become a memory,
One that feels so far away.
A vague dream you barely recall.
Questioning,
Was it ever really my life at all?

<u>Words</u>

Words are words,
Even if what they hold aren't true.
You can't control what people choose to believe,
Or the views they have of you.
You are who you are,
And you know what's true.
But you are stronger than those words.
Those words don't define you,
Even if people believe them to be true.
You only have you,
And the ones who truly love you.
Let those words go,
As you exhale your breath.
Say goodbye to the power they hold.
You are you,
You will get through.

Not Okay

I don't know what it feels like to drown,
But somehow, I feel I do.
The lump in my throat.
The knot in my stomach.
The wound in my back,
Still fresh.
Then there is the cloud,
That follows me all day,
Everyday.
The sun comes out but I still can't see,
It's all dark in here,
For me.
I'll put on a smile and pretend I'm fine,
All while I'm struggling inside.
It's so easy to let go,
And so much harder
To hold on.
I made a promise to myself,
That I wouldn't let this destroy me.
So, I'll try.
Lastly,
One more thing I have to say,
Before I'll be on my way.
It's okay,
To not be okay.

To Fight For Love

I thought you'd fight for me.
But,
Perhaps I was lied to by books, movies, and tv.
Instead, you fled the country,
Months abroad.
Many flights,
And sights to see.
Barely a conversation,
Only a few words.
Uncertainty.
I realized during that time,
I was never to you,
What you were to me.

Smile

To the broken woman who finally got her smile
back,
Never let anyone or anything ever take it away.
I always knew you'd be okay.
Being lost wasn't a place to stay.
A heart like yours,
Good things will come.
And you'll no longer have to wonder why
It wasn't enough.
Because it always was.
You are beautiful,
Inside and out.
So please smile,
And never let it fade.
It's too bright,
To ever let it be taken away.

The Difference

I cried the whole way home,
Tears after tears.
I taste the salt.
And smell like you,
I wish it didn't kill me to see you hurt.
I wish your arms didn't feel like my safe place,
When they no longer are.
I see your pain,
And
I want to carry it for you,
But I can't.
It's no longer mine to hold.
And then,
At that moment I realized
The difference between,
Me,
And you.
I would have always tried to take the pain away,
So, you'd be okay.

Depression

It's darkness.
It's grey.
Its heaviness,
And its hold on you.
It consumes your energy,
And no sleep satisfies it.
It doesn't know happy,
Only sadness.
It wants you all to itself,
Likes to isolate its prey.
It pushes you into the deep,
Dark hole.
Away from the light.
Away from any feeling,
You are numb,
One of its favourite ways.
It'll keep you as long as it can,
Until help,
Fights it away.

Fade Away

Sometimes I wonder how it would feel
To fade away.
To go to a place where things no longer feel so
heavy.
A place where I'm no longer in pain.
A place where I'm free,
Free from the thoughts,
The memories.
A place where I no longer feel so empty.
I feel dead while I'm alive,
Would I finally feel alive if I were dead?
I don't want to die,
But sometimes I don't know how I'll make it
through.
I just want to be able to breathe again,
Let my lungs fill up, fully.
I'll never give up,
You don't need to worry,
But please know what I carry is heavy.
I'm trying my best,
Like I always do.

Takes Two

They say a relationship takes two,
So here I am
Accepting my part.
Taking some of the blame
Of everything that fell apart.
I'm sorry I made you feel that you were not enough.
That the only way for you to feel alive,
Was with someone else's touch.
I see my faults,
Trust me.
I really do.
But,
Please don't question.
The way I loved you.

Grieving

When will I stop grieving?
Grieving you.
Grieving us.
The life I imagined.
The life events I thought we'd have.
You next to me.
The sound of a baby's first cry.
Becoming a mother
With you.
Becoming a father,
With me.
So many dreams,
I never got to see
Come to reality.
So many memories,
We didn't get to have.
Too much grieving to do,
Not only losing you.
But
Losing the chance,
Of what I thought this could be.
The lifetime of you,
And me.
Moments,
And their memories.

<u>Things</u>

You might have those things,
But things are all they'll ever be.
I have my strength,
Power
A heartbeat.
I have my friends and family.
In the end,
It's all we ever,
Really need.

A Picturesque

I've always seen this picture.
A picturesque of what my life would be.
But,
Here I am.
And it's not at all what I thought it would be.
Was I lost then?
And now I'm found...
Or am I lost all over again?
Nothing makes sense,
In a world where I want to understand.
I try to pretend I'll stay in the present,
All while I clutch onto the past, future, and my lies.
Maybe my expectations
Took me to places I couldn't reach.
I try so hard to grasp on,
To anything,
Anything to make sense of this.
And then it hits me all again.
I'm this beautiful mess,
In this chaotic world,
Of broken hearts and dreams.
Just trying to find my place.
A lost soul,
Who's just trying to make it,
Make it in this broken world.

A True Love Story

My story is out there being written.
And one day
I will get to have the story
The one,
I know I can.
The one,
With the happy ending.
The one,
Where someone loves me,
The way I love them.

Walls

I stand here,
Looking at walls.
Solid walls.
Walls I don't know if I'll be able to break.
Walls I am so scared to let down.
These walls keep me safe,
But they also don't let me break free.
A part of me wants to stay,
Stay between the walls.
Safe.
But,
How can I truly live my life,
Confined
My heart would be safe.
I don't know if it can bare to break.
So maybe I'll just stay,
Stay here for a while.
And hopefully one day,
These four walls,
Won't stand so tall.

Some Days

Some days,
Like today,
I feel lost.
Unsure of my purpose,
Unsure of the reasons,
The reasons to be.
Lost,
In a world that seems like a maze.
Thinking and thinking,
But paralyzed by those very thoughts.
Thinking and thinking,
A mind full of thoughts,
But I still can't seem to find a reason.
So instead,
I'll try to sleep to quiet my mind.
To have a moment,
A moment of peace.

I Close My Eyes

I feel the sunshine glistening down, touching my
skin.
It spreads warmth, a kind of warmth that makes you
feel alive.
I sit there, and let it continue to warm my skin.
I feel at peace.
At this very moment, the world is quiet.
No longer a strong roar of chaos in my head,
The worries vanish as the sun continues to warm
my skin.
I close my eyes.
I feel happy.
Happiness from a place I've never felt before, a
place deep inside.
All the fears, worries, doubts, and pain fade away.
Right now, they don't consume me, nor do they
hold control.
I feel this beauty, and not from something I see or
hear,
But from something I feel inside.
At this moment I've never felt more beautiful and
it's entirely because of who I am and not what I
need to be.
In this sun glistening minute, I find myself having
an epiphany.
I see myself, my very being as who I truly am, not
what I've made myself believe.
A worthy being, capable of more than I had ever
imagined.
The air I inhale is fresh and crisp.

I feel so alive, and not only because I have a
heartbeat.
A type of alive that not everyone feels.
Quite possibly, I needed this moment.
I needed the sun to touch my skin.
I need to feel the warmth of this beautiful world to
unlock the beauty in me.

Vows to myself

I vow to never beg for a man to love me.
I vow to never beg for a man to stay.
I vow to set boundaries.
I vow to trust my instincts.
I vow to stick up for myself.
I vow to always try my best.
I vow to put myself first, always.
I vow to not lose myself for another person.
I vow to always carry on, no matter how painful it may be.
I vow to stop fearing losing people; I am the only person I need.

Waves

The water will be still,
I float,
I feel the sunshine on my skin.
I feel warmth,
Hope.
Then come the waves.
They come crashing without a warning.
Suddenly,
The still water seems like a dream.
The waves carry me into the deep sea.
The deep sea of pain, betrayal, and memories.

Forget Me

I'm terrified.
Terrified of letting go,
And moving on.
However,
I can't let you be a ghost of the past,
Constantly haunting me.
To move on,
Means it's over.
Really over.
I'm not sure I'm ready,
But I'm not sure I'll ever be.
You might just always have a little part of me.
I'm scared to be me.
A me without you.
I'm scared I'll forget you.
But more so,
I'm terrified of the day,
You forget me.

Aftertaste

Bittersweet,
The bitter reality,
Yet the sweetness you remember.
The sweetness in letting go,
To rediscover.
Yet the bitterness of hurt.
The aftertaste,
That always comes after.

A Signature

A signature.
Signed,
Official.
You think you'd feel happier,
Yet, sadness creeps in.
A sadness after a book is finished.
A book that you weren't quite ready to come to an end.
You take a breath,
You close it shut.
You sit,
Book in hand.
It wasn't the ending you thought,
Not the way you expected the book to end.
Questioning the words written.
Yet, accepting the story's been written,
Sold,
And spoken.

<u>Closure</u>

Closure,
The final door being shut.
Then sealed.
Forever.
It's time to forget,
Forgive.
And move forward.
Letting go of the sealed door,
And,
Everything that lies behind it.

Breaking Down Boxes

I put myself into a box.
That box is what I was known for.
Until,
The box was broken.
Now in pieces.
Suddenly,
I'm free.
No longer in a box.
But with freedom, comes uncertainty.
The box was all I've known for so long.
It's who I was,
How I was remembered.
All I was able to see.
How do I be,
Me?
Me without the box I was in.
The box I knew.
The box you knew.
The box that was home for so long.

Healing

Healing is a journey.
First, the wound is fresh, it hurts.
Constantly stinging with pain.
A constant reminder it's there,
It's letting you know.
"Please help me" it whispers.
And then it shouts.
With time, the pain lessens.
The stinging becomes something that only hurts to touch.
You feel fine as you walk amongst your day,
But then you hit it.
And suddenly,
The pain becomes unbearable,
Again.
You scream.
You cry.
It's all too much.
Why oh, why?
But again,
It gets better and better with time.
Again, you walk amongst your day.
And you feel okay.
You look down at the scar you have,
And remember the day,
The wound.
You feel sad as memories flood in your mind.
But no longer do you feel that unbearable pain.
Although you feel sad as you recall the day.
You feel proud,
Of the healing that has come to play.

With time,
Years pass,
Your life changes.
Yet sometimes,
Maybe only once in a rare while will you see the
scar.
Really see it.
And reflect on it.
Or maybe it's when someone asks about how it
came to be.
You look down take a breath and tell them about the
scar, and the day it became a part of you.
And for the first time,
You don't feel pain,
Sadness or despair.
You feel gratitude.
The scar reminds you of who you are,
What you've overcome.
That you can love.
That you,
Yes, you,
Are human.

Everything Will Be Okay

A soft breeze,
The sound of cars.
The sun glistening on your skin.
As you take a breath,
Your chest raises,
Then falls.
You are alive.
In that moment,
You realize you're okay.
Everything will be okay.

Undressed

To the woman you were,
From the woman you are.
You undressed.
Leaving the dark, empty shell behind.
You made it back to the light.
You made it.

__Closing Remarks__

It's been a few years since I wrote most of the
writings you've just read.
You might wonder why not just leave the past in the
past instead of bringing it back to the surface.
For so long I lost myself,
My power,
My voice.
Through healing,
I've gotten to this place.
Where I'm no longer
Small,
Scared.
Or broken.
This is me reclaiming what was taken.
Grabbing my power and holding it in my hands.
I wanted to share my light,
That came from such darkness.
Be a breath of fresh air,
When I once couldn't breathe.
I wanted to be proof that you can heal.
Love,
Grow,
And be happy,
Again.
Because, here's the truth.
And please remember these words,
I'm about to tell you.
If I can make it through.
So can you.

Printed in the USA
CPSIA information can be obtained
at www.ICGtesting.com
LVHW071639261023
762250LV00019B/546